<The Power of CODING/>

The Power of JavaScript

Derek Miller

Cavendish Square
New York

Published in 2018 by Cavendish Square Publishing, LLC
243 5th Avenue, Suite 136, New York, NY 10016

First Edition

Website: cavendishsq.com

This publication represents the opinions and views of the author based on his or her personal
experience, knowledge, and research. The information in this book serves as a general
guide only. The author and publisher have used their best efforts in preparing this book and
disclaim liability rising directly or indirectly from the use and application of this book.

All websites were available and accurate when this book was sent to press.

Library of Congress Cataloging-in-Publication Data

Names: Miller, Derek.
Title: The power of JavaScript / Derek Miller.
Description: New York : Cavendish Square Publishing, 2018. | Series: The
power of coding | Includes bibliographical references and index.
Identifiers: ISBN 9781502634160 (pbk.) |ISBN 9781502629449
(library bound) | ISBN 9781502629456 (ebook)
Subjects: LCSH: JavaScript (Computer program language)--Juvenile literature. | HTML (Document
markup language)--Juvenile literature. | Internet programming--
Juvenile literature. | Web sites--Authoring programs--Juvenile literature.
Classification: LCC QA76.73.J39 2018 | DDC 005.2/762--dc23

Editorial Director: David McNamara
Editor: Caitlyn Miller
Copy Editor: Rebecca Rohan
Associate Art Director: Amy Greenan
Designer: Joe Parenteau
Production Coordinator: Karol Szymczuk
Photo Research: J8 Media

Printed in the United States of America

\<Contents/\>

```
=b.nodeName.toLowerCase();return("input"===c||"but
{return"form"in b?b.parentNode&&b.disabled===!1?"la
b.disabled===a:b.isDisabled===a||b.isDisabled!==!a&
}}function pa(a){return ia(function(b){return b=+b,
le(g--)c[e=f[g]]&&(c[e]=!(d[e]=c[e]))})})}function
gName&&a}c=ga.support={},f=ga.isXML=function(a){var
HTML"!==b.nodeName},m=ga.setDocument=function(a){va
be&&g.documentElement?(n=g,o=n.documentElement,p=!f
ener?e.addEventListener("unload",da,!1):e.attachEve
){return a.className="i",!a.getAttribute("className
endChild(n.createComment("")),!a.getElementsByTagNa
ementsByClassName),c.getById=ja(function(a){return
ntsByName(u).length}),c.getById?(d.filter.ID=functio
Attribute("id")===b}},d.find.ID=function(a,b){if("un
tById(a);return c?[c]:[]}}):(d.filter.ID=function(a)
ned"!=typeof a.getAttributeNode&&a.getAttributeNode
"undefined"!=typeof b.getElementById&&p){var c,d,e,f
d"),c&&c.value===a)return[f];e=b.getElementsByName(
&&c.value===a)return[f]}return[]}}),d.find.TAG=c.get
f b.getElementsByTagName?b.getElementsByTagName(a):
=[],e=0,f=b.getElementsByTagName(a);if("*"===a){whi
f},d.find.CLASS=c.getElementsByClassName&&function(a
return b.getElementsByClassName(a)},r=[],q=[],(c.qs
hild(a).innerHTML="<a id='"+u+"'></a><select id='"+
n></select>",a.querySelectorAll("[msallowcapture^='
ectorAll("[selected]").length||q.push("\\["+K+"*(?:
||q.push("~="),a.querySelectorAll(":checked").lengt
th||q.push(".#.+[+~]")}),ja(function(a){a.innerHTML
bled'><option/></select>";var b=n.createElement("in
etAttribute("name","D"),a.querySelectorAll("[name=d
lectorAll(":enabled").length&&q.push(":enabled",":d
torAll(":disabled").length&&q.push(":enabled",":dis
matchesSelector=Y.test(s=o.matches||o.webkitMatches
tchesSelector))&&ja(function(a){c.disconnectedMatch
length&&new RegExp(q.join("|")),r=r.length&&new Reg
||Y.test(o.contains)?function(a,b){var c=9===a.nod
!(!d||1!==d.nodeType||!(c.contains?c.contains(d):a
d)))}:function(a,b){if(b)while(b=b.parentNode)if(b==
1=!0,0;var d=!a.compareDocumentPosition-!b.compare
wnerDocument||b)?a.compareDocumentPosition(b):1,1&d
||a.ownerDocument===v&&t(v,a)?-1:b===n||b.ownerDoc
```

<Chapter One/>

The History of JavaScript

JavaScript is the most widely used programming language in the world. It is an essential component of most websites—a fact that has earned it the nickname "the language of the web." It is also used to develop applications (apps) for phones and other devices. Despite its high profile, JavaScript was designed and created in just ten days by one person: Brendan Eich. Although he did not know it at the time, his creation would revolutionize the way that people use the internet and make web pages. Since its creation

Opposite: JavaScript is written using letters, numbers, punctuation marks, and special characters.

in 1995, JavaScript has been an integral part of web development. Millions of programmers use JavaScript to do their jobs and develop the programs that shape our lives. But before we look at the important ways that JavaScript is used today, let's look at its fascinating history in the early years on the internet.

In 1995, the internet was still in its infancy. The World Wide Web had just been made available to the public in 1991, and it was still quite slow and tedious to use. Internet browsers—used to view web pages—were still rudimentary and had long load times. To open a new web page generally took at least thirty seconds, if not more, on the telephone-line modems people used to access the internet. Because of this, filling out forms on the internet (for instance, to open a new email account), was a painstaking process. If you forgot to fill in a field, you would have to wait while your computer sent a request to the server. The server would then send a response back pointing out the error. In this way, even the most basic online tasks became tiresome because of the need for your computer to communicate over the slow internet to accomplish anything.

JavaScript was created to remedy this issue. It enabled web pages to check to see if every required field was filled in before sending a request to the server. This meant that if users left a field blank, they could be informed before the lengthy communication between their computer (also known as the client) and the server began.

JavaScript became the first popular client-side programming language. Its widespread adoption marked a fundamental shift in internet history. Tasks could now be accomplished both client-side and server-side with ease. The functions of JavaScript quickly grew, and it was soon used for many things other than simply checking forms and other basic tasks. It allowed websites to become more interactive and paved the way for the modern landscape of the internet.

Browser Warfare

The history of JavaScript is bound up with the so-called browser war, a competition between Microsoft and Netscape to become the dominant web browser supplier to the world. Netscape was the early dominant force in the fledgling web browser market. It released its first browser in 1994 and rapidly took a majority of the browser market. It seemed poised to become the unquestioned leader of the industry.

However, in 1995, Microsoft responded. Already a tech giant due to the popularity of Microsoft Windows, Microsoft's founder Bill Gates intended to take over the browser market as well. The company launched Internet Explorer, a new browser, to compete with Netscape Navigator. It began including the software

Microsoft founder Bill Gates

for free with Windows, the **operating system** that came with nearly all computers at the time.

The war was over quickly. Within five years, Windows controlled 95 percent of the browser market. Netscape was destroyed. Microsoft's hardball tactics had worked, but they would soon be used against the tech giant. The Justice Department of the United States went after the company for being a monopoly and unfairly using Windows to crush competitors. Netscape's CEO was called to the stand during the proceedings, and Microsoft was vilified in court.

At one point, Microsoft was ordered by the court to temporarily remove Internet Explorer from the basic version of Windows. Microsoft lawyers responded by arguing that Internet Explorer was an integral part of Windows and difficult to remove. However, the judge, Thomas Jackson, noted that he had uninstalled it in less than two minutes by himself and criticized the company's lawyers. In the end, Judge Jackson found that Microsoft was a monopoly and the company should be split into two separate companies: one focused on Windows, the other on software such as Internet

Explorer and Word. It was a momentous decision that might have had far-reaching consequences.

However, it was overturned when Microsoft's lawyers appealed the decision. Judge Jackson was also rebuked over his handling of the case and obvious disdain for Microsoft's arguments. The appellate court ruled that Microsoft was indeed a monopoly, but it need not split into two companies. It was a ruling that changed the history of computing technology.

JavaScript's Birth

The events of the browser war would shape JavaScript during its foundational years. Brendan Eich was a Netscape employee and created JavaScript in 1995. It was originally called LiveScript, but the name was changed just before release. A completely different programming language by the name of Java had gained popularity at the time. Netscape hoped that

Netscape Navigator's popularity plummeted with the release of Microsoft's Internet Explorer.

Brendan Eich

○ ○ ○

Brendan Eich was in the middle of his career when he invented JavaScript in 1995. He had previously worked at Silicon Graphics for seven years and spent three years at MicroUnity Systems Engineering before joining the team at Netscape. At Silicon Graphics, he had built new programming languages for the company. He had even built programming languages while he attended college to hone his understanding of programming **syntax**. It was these experiences that allowed him to create JavaScript in just ten days in 1995—an astonishing accomplishment.

In 1998, Eich took a leading role in Netscape's new project Mozilla. The name Mozilla was an early name for Netscape's browser, used by employees before the product was released as Netscape Navigator. The word was a combination of "Mosaic" (the leading browser when Netscape Navigator launched in 1994) and "killer"—the intended goal of the new program. But in 1998, Mosaic was long dead. Mozilla was supposed to support Netscape's new approach to releasing both the browser and its code for free to the general public. It was a bold experiment to promote transparency and harness the public to make improvements to already existing programs.

However, Netscape went on to lose the browser war, and its popularity continued to decline. AOL, the owner of Netscape, largely stopped supporting its development in 2003. This led to the launch of the nonprofit Mozilla Foundation as an independent organization with Mozilla as a subsidiary. The following year, Mozilla released Firefox—a new browser based on Netscape Navigator's code that was also **open source**, meaning its code was available to the public. Soon after, Eich was promoted to chief technology officer (CTO), an executive position that focuses on the development of new technology. He remained in that role for ten years.

In 2014, Eich was promoted to chief executive officer (CEO) of Mozilla. However, he was soon struck by a major scandal that made headlines around the country. It came out that he had donated $1,000 to support a controversial **referendum** in 2008. The referendum, called Proposition 8, sought to ban same-sex marriage in California. It passed at the time, but the marriage ban was later overturned by the California Supreme Court on the grounds that it unnecessarily stripped rights from a "disfavored group" to please the majority.

Even though a majority of Californians had supported Proposition 8 in 2008 like Eich did, his donation was wildly unpopular. He became the target of intense and sustained criticism. The tech industry has a reputation for supporting gay rights, and many people lambasted Eich, including some of his own employees. As a result, less than two weeks after his promotion, Eich stepped down as CEO. His resignation raised a number of ethical issues. Many questioned whether CEOs ought to be held accountable for private actions, such as donating to a political campaign. Others saw it as evidence that the distinction between work and home life was breaking down—a troubling sign for those who valued their private lives as much as their career. It remains a thorny issue of privacy and, to many people, bigotry.

Eich's career did not end with his public resignation, however. In 2015, he founded a **start-up** named Brave Software that aims to make the internet safer and faster for its users. He remains its CEO today.

Brendan Eich

by naming its own language JavaScript, it too would surge in popularity, despite the fact that the two were unrelated. It was a decision that still causes confusion to this day among people unfamiliar with programming.

JavaScript did become popular with its release in 1995, and Microsoft responded by using a clone of JavaScript—which it called JScript—in its new version of Internet Explorer. While JScript was intended to be a clone of JavaScript, the two diverged slightly. Furthermore, a very similar programming language known as ScriptEase was also in use at the time. This presented a serious problem for website developers at the time. Many websites could only run well on Internet Explorer or Netscape as a result, not on both. In fact, at this time it was common for individual websites to display a logo saying "best run on Netscape" or "best run on Internet Explorer."

Needless to say, this situation was far from ideal. People had to switch between the two browsers to surf the web effectively or resign themselves to not viewing some websites. The internet seemed poised for a permanent split due to the browser war.

Consequently, Netscape began working on standardizing the new languages. They submitted JavaScript 1.1 to the European Computer Manufacturers Association (ECMA) as a proposed standard to be used across companies. Programmers representing both Netscape and Microsoft, as well as other companies, met to create a new standard that would be adopted by all of them. The result was ECMAScript—a programming language that standardized the basics of JavaScript and JScript. While both of these languages continued to exist and built on the core of ECMAScript, there was now a standard that all websites could use. It was an important step for both JavaScript and the internet, as it made it easier for websites to be **compatible** with both Netscape Navigator and Internet Explorer.

The World Wide Web

Before moving on to the next chapter in JavaScript's history, it is necessary to look at the history of website development in general. The World Wide Web was invented in 1989 by computer scientist Tim Berners-Lee. He programmed the first internet browser the following year. He called the browser the WorldWideWeb—at the time, his browser was the only way to access the internet.

Berners-Lee invented three different technologies that remain the foundation of the web today:

1. HTTP (HyperText Transfer Protocol): a system that allows websites to link to one another.
2. URI (Uniform Resource Identifier): a unique name that denotes a resource on the web. One kind of URI is a website's URL, or address.
3. HTML (Hypertext Markup Language): the language used to format web pages.

Taken together, these three innovations laid the groundwork for the internet of today. At the time, his idea was not immediately praised. In fact, his boss wrote a note on his proposal for the World Wide Web that said simply, "vague but exciting." Nevertheless, Berners-Lee was given time to work on his project.

Over the next few years, the popularity of the World Wide Web skyrocketed. This was doubtlessly a result of Berners-Lee's determination to see his creation be free and open to the public. He encouraged his employer to make the web available to everyone and not to retain any control.

Since its earliest days, the most basic language of the web has been HTML. In fact, websites are simply documents in HTML. You likely view them through a browser, which links them to other websites, fills them with images, animates their contents, and changes them as you interact with them (almost always via JavaScript). But you could simply open a text document and see the exact same website in its HTML format. HTML documents are plain text. Through their words and numbers, they spell out just how a website will appear when it is opened in a browser.

HTML is not a programming language. Programming languages must contain instructions that are then completed. HTML simply marks up data to define what it is. As its name states, it is a markup language. Using tags (which function as commands) like <header> and <link>, HTML structures web pages. These tags make it possible for your browser to display the data correctly. But despite the fact it is not a programming language, HTML is a cornerstone of the internet.

DHTML and DOM

Websites can be built just using HTML, but those websites are **static**. When you click on a link, the whole web page reloads. The viewer cannot interact with the website. It is impossible to create tabs or other basic functions that we now expect to see on the web.

JavaScript solved this problem. As a client-side programming language, it allowed the website to change without a request being sent to the server.

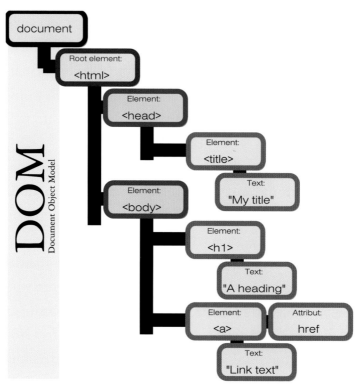

The Document Object Model (DOM) structures documents. This is an example of a simple HTML document.

As a result, the new concept of DHTML (Dynamic HyperText Markup Language) took off in 1997 with the release of Internet Explorer 4. The same year, Netscape Navigator 4 was released. Both browsers used DHTML, but they did so in different ways. Once again, it proved difficult for websites to be designed to work in both browsers.

DHTML is not a programming or markup language. Instead, it is a collection of technologies (chiefly HTML and JavaScript) that allow websites to be more interactive and dynamic. For instance, when you move your cursor over a button and the appearance of the button changes, it is DHTML that makes this possible. Before the advent of JavaScript and DHTML, this didn't happen.

To combat the rise of two different versions of DHTML, the World Wide Web Consortium (W3C) stepped in. Founded by Berners-Lee (who still heads it), the W3C recommended that browsers adopt the Document Object Model (DOM) to standardize DHTML across different browsers. The DOM relates to another markup language: XML. XML stands for eXtensible Markup Language, a text format used to store and transport data. The XML format is datacentric. It is concerned with accurately recording data. This is different from HTML, which focuses on displaying data on a web page. As a result, both markup languages are often used on the same web page.

Like DHTML, the DOM is not a programming language. It provides structure for HTML and XML documents. According to the DOM, HTML and XML documents are represented as a structured group of nodes and objects. The DOM provides a way to categorize and map the documents. Due to this mapping, JavaScript is able to manipulate any component of the complex HTML and XML documents.

The Final Piece of the Puzzle

So far, we have looked at both HTML and JavaScript. They remain the foundation of most websites to this day. But there is one missing piece we have not looked at: Cascading Style Sheets (CSS). CSS is the last of three languages that define the World Wide Web today. CSS is a style sheet language, and as its name suggests, it focuses on the presentation of a document (in practice, almost always an HTML document).

CSS allows web developers to quickly and easily format a website to look more appealing. Using CSS, they can manipulate color, font, font size, margins, and more. While HTML is capable of doing much of this work, it does not do so efficiently. CSS allows you to format things like headings, links, and backgrounds across all the many web pages that make up a website. To do the same thing in HTML, you would have to format each HTML document individually.

For instance, if you wanted every paragraph on a website to have text that was blue, centered in the middle, and the size of twelve pixels, you could write the following code:

```
p {
    font-size: 12px;

    color: blue;

    text-align: center;
}
```

There is no quick way to accomplish the same task in HTML.

Ajax

With the creation of CSS in 1996 and the DOM in 1998, the stage was set for a revolution. JavaScript had allowed websites to become more and more dynamic and interactive. Bodies like the W3C and the ECMA had also managed to create standards that were widely adopted and allowed websites to be compatible across different browsers. Websites—once static pages—were growing more sophisticated all the time. Previously, desktop applications had far surpassed the capabilities of websites, but this was soon to change.

In 2004, Google released Gmail, an email service, soon followed by Google Maps. The two websites were capable of far more than was typical of the time. Others soon followed Google's lead, and website functionality increased like never before. In 2005, interface designer and information architect Jesse James Garrett coined the term Ajax (Asynchronous JavaScript and XML) to describe the way that these new sites worked.

Ajax is not a programming language. Instead, it is a way that a website can access a web server. It allows websites to communicate with a server in the background. This in turn lets websites update what they display in real time, without the need for the website to refresh. Nowadays, Ajax is used all the time by websites we visit every day. It is how Facebook and other sites can have a never-ending stream of up-to-date information. As you read one comment, more load below it so that you can scroll down and see new content. It is Ajax that makes this possible. Before the advent of Ajax, you had to refresh a web page to see new content.

The word "asynchronous" as used in Ajax means that all of the activity is happening in the background. JavaScript is used to send a request to the server—in the case of Facebook, this request occurs when you scroll down and more content is needed. The server sends a response back, and this response is read by JavaScript and able to be displayed immediately in the browser.

Web 2.0

Around the same time, a man named Tim O'Reilly said that a fundamental reshaping of the web was underway. He referred to this new web as Web 2.0. The static web pages of old were being replaced by interactive ones—often based on collective intelligence and user engagement, like Wikipedia. Blogging became popular and replaced the old idea of personal web pages. Facebook was founded the same year as

O'Reilly began talking about Web 2.0. The web that we are familiar with today was taking shape.

The technological bedrock of Web 2.0 was Ajax. It is what allowed websites to be so dynamic and interactive. Ajax was only made possible because of JavaScript. JavaScript, running on the client side rather than on a server, allowed web pages to change constantly with user input.

Tim O'Reilly defines Web 2.0 in the following way:

Web 2.0 is the network as platform, spanning all connected devices; Web 2.0 are those that make the most of the intrinsic advantages of that platform: delivering software as a continually-updated service that gets better the more people use it, consuming and remixing data from multiple sources, including individual users, while providing their own data and services in a form that allows remixing by others, creating network effects through an "architecture of participation," and going beyond the page metaphor of Web 1.0 to deliver rich user experiences.

Since 2005, websites have continued to increase in complexity. But the ideas of collaboration and a rich user experience have remained the same. Even the

The iPhone, released in 2007, was the first smartphone that looks like today's smartphones.

technology of Ajax has remained constant, although it has changed to some degree in its execution.

The Smartphone Revolution

The next great step forward in technology was the rise of smartphones. Smartphones developed gradually with the rise in popularity of both mobile phones and personal digital assistants (hand-held devices that could send emails and connect to the internet). The two devices were combined into one device—capable of placing calls and connecting to the internet.

Early smartphones looked quite different from what we are accustomed to today. They often had small keyboards and pens attached. The screens were colorless and difficult to navigate. That all changed in 2007 with the release of the iPhone. The new innovation by Apple sent shockwaves across the tech world. Its large touchscreen and streamlined design signaled a shift in the industry. Even though the iPhone was largely rejected by businesses at the time in favor of older models of smartphones, it shaped the way that the world saw connectivity.

A year after the release of the iPhone, Google released the Android mobile operating system. Like the iPhone, it was for use on devices with large touchscreens like the ones we use today. The struggle between Apple and Google (as well as other smartphone companies) would set the stage for the so-called smartphone wars, which began in 2009 and continue to this day. Companies secured patents for technologies they used in their phones and sued competitors in courts around the world for patent infringement.

At the same time, titans like Apple and Samsung competed to sell the most phones and expand their customer base. In 2011, just 35 percent of Americans owned a smartphone according to the Pew Research Center. Today, more than 75 percent do. The rapid

Facebook and JavaScript

○ ○ ○

You've almost certainly heard of Facebook, and you might be one of the hundreds of millions of people who use it every day. But what you might not know is just how important the company is to the modern landscape of JavaScript. Before we look at the specifics of their contributions to JavaScript, let's look at their more humble beginnings as a company.

Facebook was founded in 2004 by Mark Zuckerberg, then a student at Harvard University. The site's popularity expanded extraordinarily quickly. Within a month, half of Harvard's undergraduates had accounts. In 2005, it had six million users. By March 2017, there were nearly two billion.

Facebook became one of the most highly valued companies in the world. At the beginning of 2017, the value of its stock was valued at $381 billion. With its meteoric rise, Facebook has branched out from the world of social media into different areas. The company bought popular messaging service WhatsApp in 2014 and is heavily involved in the field of virtual reality.

In 2013, Facebook released **React**—a JavaScript **library**. JavaScript libraries aim to make coding simpler and easier. They often include prewritten chunks of JavaScript that developers can use and manipulate without starting from scratch. While they still require a detailed knowledge of the programming language to use them, they can save programmers time and energy. It is also possible for websites to use more than one JavaScript library. In fact, most large websites use many different libraries to achieve different goals and solve different problems that might present themselves.

React is primarily built for the creation of user interfaces, the appearance of some technology that the user then interacts with. For a website, this includes features like navigation bars and input fields, which the user interacts with to accomplish tasks.

According to its creators, the purpose of React is to "[encourage] the creation of reusable **UI** components which present data that changes over time." Think about Facebook's user interface. There are many different scrolling sections and links that make up a very complex display. Facebook uses React to make manipulating this user interface as simple as possible. Without React, you can build a site like Facebook using JavaScript, but it is a much more time-consuming task to create and maintain it as the user interface changes over time.

According to Facebook, React also has the added benefit of helping developers improve their products beyond simplifying the creation of its user interface. According to their official blog, this is because

> React forces us to break our applications down into discrete components, each representing a single view. These components make it easier to iterate on our products, since we don't need to keep the entire system in our head in order to make changes to one part of it.

In 2015, with the release of **React Native**, a JavaScript **framework** that focuses on the creation of phone apps, Facebook expanded its reach even further into the world of JavaScript and coding resources. It remains to be seen how much more the company will do in this domain.

expansion of this market has had a huge effect on the programming world. The development of smartphone apps has become a significant industry around the globe.

Mobile app development has been greatly influenced by the two main mobile operating systems: Apple's iOS (which is restricted to Apple devices) and Google's Android (used by nearly every phone manufacturer except for Apple). In the beginning, apps could not be written in the same programming language and run on both iOS and Android. It was a situation reminiscent of the browser wars, when websites had to choose between running well on Netscape Navigator or Internet Explorer.

Android apps were typically written in Java, while iOS apps were written using Objective-C. The two different programming languages made development across both operating systems costly and time consuming. To this day, apps are often released on one platform before being reworked and released on the other.

JavaScript Conquers the Phone

In the beginning, the closest you could come to creating an app with JavaScript was a mobile web app. Despite their name, these kinds of apps are not truly applications at all. Instead, they are web pages, viewed in a browser, which seek to emulate the style and layout of an app. They cannot be downloaded from an app store, and they require a browser to open them.

But this changed in 2008. A company by the name of Nitobi Software developed a mobile application development framework called PhoneGap. It allows developers to create phone apps using JavaScript, HTML, and CSS—the three languages of website development. The apps can then run on both Android and iOS devices without the need to program the app in two different programming languages.

This was a massive step forward. It opened up the new arena of mobile app development to JavaScript, the old standard of website development. The many programmers who already knew the languages necessary to create websites could now begin work on mobile apps, without needing to learn Java or Objective-C.

PhoneGap creates hybrid apps rather than **native** apps. Hybrid apps are coded similarly to websites and then packaged in a native container so that they can be downloaded from the app store and access hardware like the phone camera. One drawback of PhoneGap, and other hybrid app development frameworks like it, is that they can perform poorly when compared to native apps. Apps coded in Java or Objective-C, depending on the operating system, tend to run faster than PhoneGap apps. This can be a significant drawback, and it is a concern that companies have to weigh against the benefit of using JavaScript rather than the other programming languages.

However, recent advances mean that JavaScript can be used to make truly native apps and not just hybrid apps. One of the leading frameworks that makes native apps using JavaScript is React Native. React Native was created by Facebook in 2015—it was used to make

Mark Zuckerberg started Facebook in 2004. In 2015, Facebook created the JavaScript framework React Native.

Facebook's app as well as the apps of other high-profile companies like Instagram and Walmart.

With React Native, you can code in JavaScript, but when the app runs, the user interface is displayed using native components. Thanks to the framework, you no longer have to choose between a hybrid app with slower performance or a native app programmed multiple times in difficult languages such as Objective-C and Java to function on both iOS and Android.

With the rise of React Native and other frameworks like it, JavaScript is poised to expand even further into the field of app development. It is now possible for programmers to build websites and create apps using just one language. The incredible power and utility of JavaScript mean it is the most used programming language today, and consequently, it is commonly the first language that new programmers learn.

<Chapter Two/>

How It Works

How JavaScript works depends on how it is used. Originally, JavaScript was used solely for web development on the client side (also known as the **front end**). A programming language on the front end runs on the user's computer, specifically their browser. It creates and changes what appears on the computer as you browse a website. Today, JavaScript remains the only popular programming language that fills this role. This is an astonishing fact considering there are numerous popular languages used on the **back end** (or server side), such as Java, Ruby, PHP, C, and Python.

Opposite: Browsers before the era of JavaScript, like Mosaic, looked very different from what we're used to.

Back-end programming languages run on the server that hosts a website. They finish running before the website is displayed, while JavaScript can continue to work while the website is displayed. Back-end programming languages are responsible for doing the work that goes on behind the scenes. For instance, when you purchase something online, it is the back end that processes the information you entered, verifies the transaction, and begins the shipping process.

Front-End Web Development

JavaScript's reign as the most important front-end programming language is ongoing. Together with HTML and CSS, it is usually responsible for creating a website's user interface that is displayed in a browser.

To do this, JavaScript is coded directly into the HTML document that is a website. It is useful to look at the basic format of an HTML document to understand how this works. In stripped-down form, a website looks like this:

```
<!DOCTYPE html>
<html>
<head>
<title> This is displayed at the top of a browser </title>
</head>
<body>
<p >This is a paragraph.</p>
</body>
</html>
```

Let's look at the parts of this example to get a basic grasp of HTML. The line <!DOCTYPE html> clarifies that the following document is in HTML; it is at the top of most websites on the web. The <html> tag marks the beginning of what is called the root **element** of the page. At the very end of the page, the </html> signals the end of this element. In HTML (and some other languages), the back slash (/) is used to signal the end of a component. In this way, HTML tags are often spoken of as pairs, with a beginning tag, such as <html>, and an end tag, such as </html>.

Within this pair of tags are the head and body elements. The head contains metadata—or a description of the data. What is written in this element is not displayed on the actual web page itself, although the contents of the title element do appear in a tab above the web page in most modern browsers. Inside the body element, there are the contents of the web page itself. In this example, there is one paragraph that appears inside the <p> and </p> pair. Any formatting of this text would generally be done in CSS, not HTML.

The above example is written entirely in HTML. It would be a static web page of just one sentence. In order to make it more dynamic, you could insert JavaScript into the HTML. JavaScript can be in the head or the body, and it can be used for all sorts of functions. Here's an example of JavaScript used to create a button on a web page:

```
<!DOCTYPE html>
<html>
<body>
<p> What is the answer to 1+1? </p>
<p> Click on the button to find out! </p>
<button type="button" onclick="document.write(1 +
1)">Click here to show the answer.</button>
</body>
</html>
```

As you can see, most of this code is in HTML. The document type, HTML, body, and paragraph tags are all basic HTML. However, the part of the code that creates the button is written in JavaScript. This part makes the web page dynamic. When you click on the button that appears, all the text is replaced by the number "2." (JavaScript also performs the calculation of adding one plus one.)

This change takes place on the client side. That means there is no request sent to the server through the internet. This is why JavaScript is so important—it remains the only widespread language able to complete this task. Other languages could add one plus one and change the web page, but they would require the user to refresh and for there to be another request sent to the server. Here, the user's display changes instantly thanks to processes completed on their own computer.

JavaScript Basics

Adding a button to a website is a common and easy example of JavaScript, but it can accomplish a lot more. Much of JavaScript's functionality depends on the fact that it is an object-oriented programming language. This means that it uses objects to accomplish tasks. An object is a collection of data and actions that can be performed on data.

Let's look at a simple object to illustrate what an object is. Imagine you want to store data about a person. You could write the following code to do that:

```
var person = {firstName:"John", lastName:"Doe", age:17, eyeColor:"brown"};
```

Var at the beginning stands for "variable," and it declares the name of the object: person. Then, there are four different **properties**: first name, last name, age, and eye color. Properties are values. These values can be different **data types**. Here, three of the values are **strings**—or text—and one is a number, but they could also be **Booleans**. Boolean data types have the value "true" or "false." For instance, a person might have a Boolean data type specifying whether they are married or unmarried. It is either true or false.

So far, we have just looked at the different types of data that can be stored about an object. But properties can also be **methods**. Methods in JavaScript are actions that can be performed on objects. There are a huge number of methods in JavaScript since they allow you to manipulate data and give JavaScript much of its functionality. One common example used on web pages is the sort() method, which sorts the elements of an **array** (a special variable that can store more than one value). One method that acts on strings is the toUpperCase() method—it converts a string to all capital letters.

At first glance, it might looks relatively easy to write code like:

```
var person = {firstName:"John", lastName:"Doe", age:17,
eyeColor:"brown"};
```

But the syntax—or rules that govern how code is written—can take some time to master. If your code doesn't comply with JavaScript's syntax, it will not work. Let's look at some of the basic rules of writing JavaScript.

JavaScript is case sensitive, unlike some other programming languages. This means it is important whether any given character is capital or lowercase. A single mistake with regards to capitalization might render your code unusable. Capitalization is important because by convention JavaScript uses a format known as camel case. This means that compound words do not have a space between them and individual words are capitalized. In the name example, you can see this in the way that "firstName," "lastName," and "eyeColor" are written. In JavaScript, the first word is usually left lower case, but the words after it are capitalized.

There are a number of other syntax rules like this in JavaScript. For instance, semicolons must be used at the end of some lines of code, but not others. Beginning programmers often struggle to do this perfectly, and many problems can crop up as a result.

To leave a comment in your code, you put /* or // in front of the text. This allows you to leave notes to yourself or other programmers working on the project. Making sure your code is easy to understand for other people looking at it (or even yourself in the future) is an important part of being a good programmer.

All of these syntax rules can be quite overwhelming when you are learning to code. It can also be confusing because different programming languages have different rules. Often they overlap to a certain degree, but there are small differences that can make even an experienced programmer make mistakes if they are not careful.

Debugging

One of the trickiest parts of programming is debugging. Whenever you write a large block of code, it almost always has bugs. These can be mistakes in syntax— how the code is formatted—or logical mistakes. Logical mistakes can take many forms. One example is trying to call a nonexistent property. This results in an error because the property cannot be acted on if it does not exist.

Luckily, there are many tools available to help you debug your code. In fact, most internet browsers have a built-in tool for debugging JavaScript. Tools can point out mistakes in your code so that you can fix them. Some browsers can even help you improve the performance of your web page. They can analyze how long it takes each event to occur on your web page and let you pinpoint any performance issues that are leading to slow load times.

Where to Write Code

Many programmers use an Integrated Development Environment (IDE). An IDE is a program that you

Integrated Development Environments add color to your code to make it easier to see each piece.

type your code into. While it's possible to write code for a website in a simple text editor like Notepad, an IDE makes writing code a lot easier. If you forget a semicolon in Notepad, you won't notice until you go to run your code. Then, when it doesn't work, you have to search through all that you've written and try to diagnose the problem. An IDE can prevent this by pointing out when you've made a mistake like a missing semicolon or the failure to use proper capitalization.

Back-end Web Development

So far, we have mostly looked at front-end web development—which relies on HTML—but JavaScript is also used on the back end or server side. The front end is what you see when you look at a web page. In fact, you can even view the code of any website in your browser. (The steps to do so vary based on the browser you use.) Your browser will display the HTML—and almost always CSS and JavaScript as well—that is creating what you are viewing.

On the other hand, the back end functions largely behind the scenes. For instance, when you Google something, Google's server uses an algorithm to create a list of websites that match your search. This happens entirely on the back end. Google then sends you to a new web page that displays the results that were created on their server. The actions that take place on

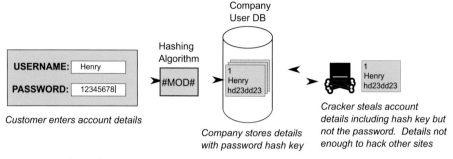

Hashing algorithms on the back end protect users' passwords.

the server aren't visible to the user. This is why the exact code of Google's search algorithm isn't known.

Databases are one of the most important parts of the back end. They can store different kinds of information that are often needed to make a website function properly. One example of commonly stored information is usernames. You might think that passwords are stored in databases as well, but in fact they almost never are. Storing passwords there would be a huge security risk if the database were compromised.

Instead, hashed passwords are generally stored on the web server. Hashed passwords are strings of random characters that are generated based on a password that you enter. Hashed passwords are like **encrypted** passwords, but encryption can be easily reversed if you have the encryption key. With hashed passwords, there is no key. Therefore, there is no easy way to generate a user's password if you gain access to the hashed password. This means that if a hacker gains access to the web server, they won't be able to gain access to anyone's account very easily.

A JavaScript **runtime** is required to execute JavaScript on the back end. On the front end, the browser handles this. By far the most popular JavaScript runtime on the back end is Node.js. It has been used by many websites of high-profile companies, including Netflix, Microsoft, and Walmart. Node.js allows you to use JavaScript on the back end to meet the needs described above, rather than a different programming language like Java or Ruby.

Libraries and Frameworks

Once you've learned the basics of JavaScript, there are many libraries and frameworks to help you build websites. The boundary between libraries and frameworks is somewhat difficult to pinpoint. In general, libraries contain JavaScript objects and functions that you can then incorporate into your own code. This is much easier than starting from scratch and trying to code everything yourself. Most websites use more than one library. On the other hand, frameworks are much more robust than libraries. They try to simplify many aspects of development, and to do this, they often use many different libraries.

APIs

○ ○ ○

One important concept in programming is that of an API (Application Program Interface). An API dictates how two software components will communicate with one another. This broad definition means that APIs are used to complete a variety of tasks. For instance, if you are developing software, you will use operating system APIs to integrate the app and the operating system. Many extensive online databases also release their own APIs to give researchers more powerful tools. For example, the Digital Public Library of America has an API that programmers can take advantage of in order to manipulate DPLA data more easily.

However, for the purposes of website development, APIs fill a particular niche that you have probably seen many times before. They allow websites to easily embed **third-party** components into your website. This is how many websites allow you to create an account using your Gmail address or Facebook account. It is also how many websites will have YouTube videos embedded in them.

Let's look at Google Maps to see how this works. To add a map with a marker on it to your website, you simply need to paste the following JavaScript into your website after completing some preparatory tasks:

```
<script async defer

 src="https://maps.googleapis.com/maps/api/
js?key=YOUR_API_KEY&callback=initMap">

</script>
```

APIs make it easy for developers to embed Google Maps into websites. Offline, Google Maps markers have even made their way into art, like this sculpture by Aram Bartholl.

Then, when your website loads, it will contain a map provided by Google Maps that has a marker at a location you previously specified. This is much easier than creating your own map and marker. And your users are also able to take advantage of the many features that Google Maps has built into it, such as directions and satellite view. This illustrates the power of APIs and the short lines of JavaScript that are used to add them to websites. With very little effort, web developers can take advantage of polished websites like Google Maps and YouTube to improve their own websites and provide difficult-to-code services like video playback and precise maps.

The most popular JavaScript library is jQuery. Like all libraries, you need to download the jQuery library or link to a Content Delivery Network (CDN) on the internet to use it. Google hosts a CDN that supplies jQuery for free. Once you have access to jQuery, you can simplify many different processes on your website. Some of the main uses of jQuery are DOM manipulation (the structure of a web page), Ajax support, and the animation of images. While jQuery has many different, discrete uses, it is still considered a library because it isn't an overarching framework that radically changes how you build a website.

Another convenient thing you can do with jQuery is create **callback** functions. Since JavaScript statements are executed line by line, errors can occur when a line of code is executed before a previous line that it depends on has finished executing. To prevent this issue, callback functions are used. A callback function allows you to specify that another function should be executed only after another one has finished. Many developers create callback functions without the aid of jQuery, but it is possible to simplify the process using a library like jQuery.

As of 2017, the most-used JavaScript framework is **AngularJS**. It is an open-source project maintained by Google, and its focus is on streamlining the creation of single-page apps using HTML and JavaScript.

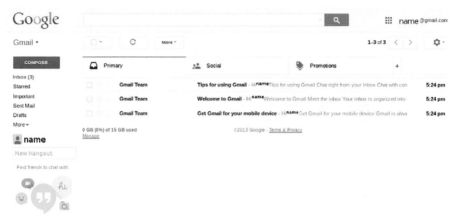

Gmail's ability to do many different things on one webpage, like look at different inboxes and draft emails, is thanks to JavaScript.

Single-page apps are single web pages that function somewhat like an app or program. They don't require loading different web pages like a traditional website made up of many different pages. For example, Gmail is a single-page app. Once you log in and access your account, you can read emails, draft them, and look through different inboxes, all without navigating to a different page.

AngularJS is more extensive than a library—its goal is to be the only resource needed to build a single-page app on the client side (it does not extend to the server side). AngularJS's website describes it in the following way:

AngularJS is a structural framework for dynamic web apps. It lets you use HTML as your template language and lets you extend HTML's syntax to express your application's components clearly and succinctly …

AngularJS is not a single piece in the overall puzzle of building the client-side of a web application. It handles all of the DOM and Ajax [code that connects different components so they become compatible] you once wrote by hand and puts it in a well-defined structure.

The chief competitor to AngularJS's popularity is React. React is a library and not a framework, but most of the time, developers use one or the other to create a website. Which one is better often depends on the exact nature of the website, although the experience of the developer also sometimes plays a role—many developers are more familiar with one over the other.

One of the primary benefits of using a framework like AngularJS is that it reduces the amount of code you have to write. It makes it unnecessary for you to handle issues like callbacks, which are a necessity if you are coding outside of a framework and can take up quite a bit of a developer's time without visibly improving a site. Frameworks can let you focus more on big picture issues like the functionality of the website and what you are trying to accomplish with it instead.

Asynchronous JavaScript

Code is often synchronous. This means it is executed in order. However, as previously mentioned, there is a major drawback with some synchronous code. It is often necessary to wait for a previous command to be executed before the next one can be completed. This can cause synchronous code to load slowly. If one process is taking a long time, execution grinds to a halt.

To get around this problem, JavaScript can be written asynchronously. You can manipulate when code is executed and ensure that slow processes don't result in long load times on your web page or application. In fact, asynchrony is so important that "asynchronous" is the "A" in Ajax. Without the ability to place asynchronous server requests—that don't make the web page wait for a response—Ajax wouldn't allow for fast, interactive web pages.

Nevertheless, the asynchronous nature of some JavaScript can be a huge headache for developers. It is difficult to write simple, direct code that is asynchronous in the correct places. In fact, the mishandling of callbacks, one important tool for asynchronous code, is one of the most common reasons for **spaghetti code**: code that is as well organized as a bowl of spaghetti.

Luckily, many JavaScript libraries and frameworks can help you avoid common problems with asynchronous code. Some JavaScript engines even include two

Hacking with JavaScript

○ ○ ○

A computer infected with ransomware.

One of the less well-known uses of JavaScript is for nefarious purposes. Malware—or malicious software—has been written completely in JavaScript on occasion. Recently, there have been two high-profile cases where JavaScript was used to attack vulnerable computers.

In 2016, a new kind of ransomware appeared on the internet. Ransomware encrypts the files on a computer and locks the owner out of them. They are unable to access the files unless they pay a ransom to the hackers. While ransomware is a typical kind of malware, this attack was notable because the ransomware was coded in JavaScript.

JavaScript was a clever choice for the malware because programs tend to trust JavaScript files. You can open such a file from an email easily, and many email clients do not warn the user that such as action is not secure. They simply run the code—and in this case that resulted in the data on the infected computers being held hostage unless the owner paid $250.

The malware was named RAA. As always, the best way to avoid infection was to not open the attachment from the original email delivering the malware. RAA was the first time that ransomware was created solely using JavaScript. But given the popularity of the language, it is unlikely to be the last.

Researchers have also used JavaScript to take over computers and phones using the so-called Rowhammer exploit. This attack relies on the hardware—or physical components—of a device rather than its programs. Usually, JavaScript from a website is forbidden from accessing the most vital memory locations of a device. This prevents websites from stealing sensitive information like passwords or taking over your computer. However, when memory locations are accessed in a certain way, there is a small chance that neighboring memory locations are changed. Rowhammer takes advantage of this fact and is capable of taking over devices by repeatedly accessing its memory until it can corrupt and take over the most important parts of the device's memory—parts that it is usually locked out of.

According to researchers, it is "the first remote software-induced hardware-fault attack." In other words, it is the first time that a program has been able to exploit a vulnerability found in the physical nature of a device from a location across the world. Other hardware-fault attacks have relied on having physical access to the device: an example is shining a laser on a device may be able to crack encryption in some cases.

Rowhammer represents a threat of the future and one reason that security researchers are so concerned about it is its use of JavaScript. There are few steps that you can take to prevent a website from running JavaScript if you have it enabled. And since the weakness it targets is in a device's hardware, no easy fix is possible.

new functions (async and await) that will simplify the task of writing asynchronous code. While the two functions have not yet been adopted by the ECMA and added to standard JavaScript, they likely will be at some point in the future.

Making Phone Apps

Coding phone apps has often been a time-consuming activity. The prevalence of iOS and Android operating systems on phones means that apps usually have to be programmed in two different programming languages. Traditionally, this was Objective-C for iOS and Java for Android. However, this has changed in recent years. Objective-C has been largely replaced by the programming language Swift. Developed by Apple in 2014, it is similar to Objective-C but tries to be simpler and easier to learn. This was a major step forward for making app development easier for companies and individuals alike.

Today, JavaScript frameworks also allow apps to be programmed in only JavaScript. By far the most popular of these frameworks is Facebook's React Native. React Native is very different from React—the JavaScript library that focuses on website interfaces. React Native is considered a framework rather than a library, and it is solely concerned with the creation of apps for iOS and Android devices—not websites.

To get started with React Native, you simply need to download the free files available on Facebook's website and ensure that you have Node.js on your computer. Then, you are ready to start coding. React's website gives the following code as an example that creates an app displaying the words "Hello world!":

```
import React, { Component } from 'react';
import { AppRegistry, Text } from 'react-native';

export default class HelloWorldApp
extends Component {
  render() {
    return (
      <Text>Hello world!</Text>
    );
  }
}
// skip this line if using Create React Native App
AppRegistry.registerComponent('HelloWorldApp', () =>
HelloWorldApp);
```

There are a number of features of JavaScript that you might recognize. Semicolons are used at the end of statements. Camel case is used in the code, and two backslashes mark the beginning of a comment in the code that is not executed. However, this is a very simple example of an app programmed with React Native. Fully developed apps can be quite complex, despite the use of a framework to simplify things.

<Chapter Three/>

Strengths and Weaknesses

JavaScript has a number of strengths and weaknesses. Some are the result of its popularity, while others are the result of its very design as a programming language. Like all programming languages, many of the design decisions that shaped the language came with benefits and drawbacks. Multiple languages can accomplish the same tasks with varying levels of difficulty—the best language to use for a project depends on your goal. However, JavaScript is unique in a number of very important ways. This is why it is the programming language most commonly used by professional developers. There is often no way to replace JavaScript—especially in web development.

Opposite: JavaScript is everywhere, including your inbox. But that doesn't mean that it's the best language for all web development.

Therefore, it is unlikely to fade in popularity any time soon. In this chapter, we look at a number of advantages and disadvantages of JavaScript.

The Only Client-Side Scripting Language

JavaScript remains the only real choice for a client-side **scripting language**. This is an absolutely essential role in website development. It is what allows your browser to change the display of a website and check that you have completed forms without sending a request to the server. The lack of such a language was the reason for JavaScript's creation, but unlike many other languages, JavaScript has never seen a serious competitor try to take its place. For this reason, JavaScript is a fixture in the realm of web development.

The benefits of such a language are multifaceted. They allow websites to be far faster and servers to be put under less stress. This is due to the fact that more can happen on the user's machine rather than through repeated communications between the client and server. Less online communication means that the user has to wait less time for the website to refresh or update as it sends requests over the internet. Instead, it can update virtually instantaneously as client-side scripts specify that the appearance should change or a request should not be made because a required form is blank.

Client-side programming languages are also a necessary component of Ajax (which is why JavaScript is the "J" in the acronym). JavaScript allows websites to update constantly behind the scenes so that components like Facebook's news feed can scroll endlessly with new content without the need for the web page to refresh. Here, too, JavaScript is impossible to replace. This benefit is hugely important. Without Ajax, the World Wide Web would be a very different place—and it is all made possible by JavaScript.

Popularity: A Blessing and a Curse

One of the chief benefits of learning JavaScript is its incredible utility. No other language can be used to do so many different things. Not only is JavaScript required to build a modern website, it can also be used to make phone apps and desktop apps if you download free, open-source frameworks.

Therefore, if you learn JavaScript well, you can complete all sorts of projects on your own. From building fully functional websites to mobile games, JavaScript can do it all.

According to surveys, JavaScript is used by a greater number of computer programmers than any other programming language. It is popular not only among front-end web developers—where it is virtually

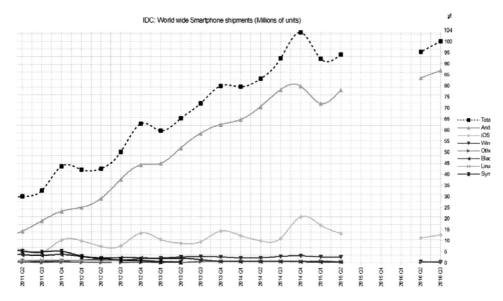

React Native allows developers to create apps for both Android and iOS phones, the two most popular operating systems for smartphones.

required—but also among back-end developers who have other options like Java. It is also gaining popularity in app creation as frameworks like React Native are refined.

This popularity comes with a number of benefits. It means that JavaScript is a popular language for programmers to learn, since it is a requirement for so many jobs. If you are expected to do anything related to website development, at least a basic knowledge of JavaScript is required. Working on the front end, a detailed knowledge of JavaScript and likely its libraries and frameworks is also needed. Consequently, there are many jobs available for someone who knows JavaScript well. While knowledge of less popular programming languages is also lucrative, there are not always hundreds of job openings at any given time for someone well-versed in these languages. For instance, more professional programmers reported using the AngularJS framework in 2016 than both Ruby and Objective-C combined, according to a survey. These survey results are stunning because the majority of people who used JavaScript did not use AngularJS. There are so many developers using JavaScript that even those who used AngularJS topped the respondents who use Ruby and Objective-C.

JavaScript's popularity is also a drawback in some ways. Widespread technologies are often the first to be targeted by hackers because of their popularity. It makes more sense to try to find vulnerabilities in common features of websites and programs—such as JavaScript—rather than rarely used features.

One of the most notorious vulnerabilities that JavaScript has is known as Cross-Site Scripting (XSS). The basic idea of cross-site scripting is rather simple—the hacker tries to get a website to execute a script that sends malicious scripts to other users of a website. You might wonder how this is possible, and the answer can be surprising.

The simplest kind of XSS attacks rely on a website's own input field, like a search bar or username field. Rather than a username, a hacker inputs code and sees if the websites executes it. If the website is secure, it will determine that it should not run the code, but if it is vulnerable, it may execute it. The hacker can then design code that directs the website to send malicious scripts to other users as well. Since these scripts come from the trusted website, they are executed by the browsers of other users.

The end result is that the attacker can access the cookies (what websites use to track visitors) and other information of innocent users who visit the affected website. In a worst-case scenario, these cookies may contain credit card numbers and other sensitive personal information. While this simple form of XSS, relying on input fields, has become so well known that almost all websites protect against it, more sophisticated XSS vulnerabilities still exist on the web. According to High-Tech Bridge, a computer-security firm, in 2015 some 80 percent of security vulnerabilities were related to XSS. Unsurprisingly, almost all XSS vulnerabilities relate to JavaScript since it is the only client-side scripting language.

Users without JavaScript

One serious drawback of JavaScript is that some users do not receive content that relies on it. The exact number of people who view websites without the enhancement of JavaScript is hard to say. One of the most rigorous studies on the issue was conducted by the British Government Digital Service in 2013. Their finding was that about 1.1 percent of users did not properly receive content that required JavaScript. Interestingly, only 0.2 percent had JavaScript disabled; JavaScript simply didn't work properly for the remaining 0.9 percent of users.

While this percent of users is quite low, it can be an extremely large number of people on a high-traffic website. For example, Facebook saw an average of 1.28 billion daily users in the first quarter of 2017. If 1.1 percent of that number could not properly see content relying on JavaScript, it would be 14 million people. However, it is interesting to note that Facebook will not even let you view the site with JavaScript disabled, most likely since it relies so heavily on Ajax. If you try to access Facebook with JavaScript disabled, the site displays a message that says "Facebook doesn't work properly without JavaScript enabled" and redirects you to the mobile site. Other popular sites like Amazon will allow you to navigate without JavaScript, since otherwise they might lose 1 percent of their customers, although some functions are lacking when it is disabled.

Because of this issue, web developers are left with a choice of whether or not to optimize websites for users without JavaScript. It can be time-consuming to ensure that a stripped-down version of a website is functional when JavaScript is disabled, but often developers will take the time to do so rather than lose approximately 1 percent of a site's traffic.

Full-Stack Web Development

There are many different parts to a fully functioning website. It is necessary to have a front end (that the user sees) and a back end (that manipulates data and handles server requests). At a large company like Facebook or Amazon, different teams of people generally work on these different parts of the website. For example, the people who manipulate and structure Facebook's databases don't work on the user interface. Each team has highly specialized skills that relate to their area of expertise. There is then an additional team with a general knowledge of the front end and back end that integrates the two parts.

The development of a typical website without the reach of Facebook is a different matter, however. On smaller websites, a single developer often designs and maintains the site. In fact, this is one of the largest fields

The term "MEAN stack" was coined in 2013, and it remains a popular way for people to design websites.

of employment related to computer programming. It is called full-stack web development. Full-stack web developers are able to work on both the front end and back end of a website. They typically have knowledge and experience with all aspects of building a website, although they may not have the specialized skills of someone who, for example, works only on databases on the back end.

A full-stack web developer needs to have a good grasp of HTML, CSS, and JavaScript—as a starting point. There are also many other languages commonly used on the back end, such as SQL and Java. One significant advantage that JavaScript has over other programming languages for a full-stack developer is that it is possible to create a website or web app using primarily JavaScript and no other languages other than HTML and CSS.

In fact, JavaScript is the only language with which it is possible to do this. The most popular free, open-source JavaScript stack is called the MEAN stack. MEAN stands for MongoDB (which handles the databases), Express.js (a web application framework), AngularJS, and Node.js. All four of these are written using JavaScript.

There are a few different advantages of using a stack written in one language. First, it is possible to use the same code on the front end and the back end. This

JavaScript, CSS, and HTML

○ ○ ○

One of JavaScript's important features is its ability to interact with CSS and HTML—the other two languages needed to create high-quality web pages. Let's look at an example of a simple web page built using HTML, CSS, and JavaScript to see how such interactions take place:

```
<!DOCTYPE html>
<html>
<head>
<style>
p {
    color: blue;
    text-align: center;
}
</style>
</head>
<body>
<p id="demo" onclick="myFunction()">Original
Paragraph.</p>
<script>
function myFunction() {
    document.getElementById("demo").innerHTML =
"Displayed after click.";
}
</script>
</body>
</html>
```

The html, head, and body tags are necessary HTML tags to structure the page. These tags organize the web page according to the DOM. Inside the HTML style tag (located in the head), you can find lines of CSS. These lines of code specify that all text inside HTML paragraph tags (<p> and </p>) is blue and centered in the middle of the page. Inside the body, there is one paragraph that is given an id of "demo" and contains the text "Original Paragraph." When a user first loads this web page, these two words (in blue at the center of the page) are all that appear.

Thus far, it appears to be a static web page. However, the JavaScript that follows makes it dynamic. The lines of code contained within the script tags interact with onclick="myFunction()" within the paragraph tags. Consequently, when the viewer clicks on the text "Original Paragraph," these two words are replaced by text reading "Displayed after click." This text is styled the same way—in blue and centered—due to the CSS at the top of the page. In this way, JavaScript is capable of interacting with HTML.

Let's look at a similar example that shows JavaScript interacting with CSS:

```
<!DOCTYPE html>
<html>
<head>
<style>
p {
    color: blue;
    text-align: center;
}
</style>
</head>
<body>
<p id="p1">Styled by CSS above</p>
<p id="p2">Style changed by JavaScript below</p>
<script>
document.getElementById("p2").style.color = "red";
document.getElementById("p2").style.textAlign = "left";
document.getElementById("p2").style.fontFamily =
"Arial";
document.getElementById("p2").style.fontSize =
"larger";
</script>
```

○ ○ ○

```
<p>This is styled by the CSS at the top.</p>
</body>
</html>
```

In this example, there are three paragraphs. The top two have ids and the bottom one does not. The first and last paragraphs are styled according to the CSS at the top: blue and centered. However, the middle paragraph "p2" is not. Its style is changed by the JavaScript. When this HTML document is opened in a browser, it will be larger, red text at the left of the page in Arial font. JavaScript was used to change the formatting first defined by CSS.

If you look at the formatting of this example, you can see differences between the CSS and JavaScript. Between the style tags, we use text-align. But between the script tags, we use textAlign— note the camel case rather than the hyphen. If you try to use the CSS syntax in the JavaScript section, it will not work. The alignment of the text will not change. This shows just how easy it is to make simple mistakes that may affect how your web page looks.

While these two examples are quite simple, the interaction of CSS, HTML, and JavaScript is extremely important to modern websites. It allows all sorts of dynamic functions that let the user interact with a responsive user interface rather than a boring, static page.

can reduce the time spent writing code in different languages to accomplish the same or similar tasks. Second, if you are just starting to learn programming, it is much easier to master JavaScript than a number of different programming languages. Third, if you are part of a team, all members of the team are working in JavaScript and can therefore collaborate more. If your stack contains a number of different languages, it is less likely all members of the team will be able to understand all of them.

The Level of Support

The popularity of JavaScript and the MEAN stack have led to another benefit of using JavaScript: there are countless resources on the web to make programming in JavaScript easier. Large communities exist where you can ask questions, and hundreds of websites have tutorials on how to reach programming goals in JavaScript.

Even after you have mastered the language, the huge number of JavaScript libraries and frameworks

jQuery is one example of a free, open-source JavaScript library that anyone can use.

that exist can simplify your life. Libraries exist that can handle of large number of specialized tasks. Additionally, many of these libraries and frameworks are open source. This means they are updated constantly by their community of users.

Rendering Concerns

One major disadvantage of using JavaScript is the fact that a website's appearance can vary depending on the browser that is used to view it. This is a headache for web developers, and the issues this causes can take an extraordinary amount of time to address. Browser rendering issues are one of the factors that make a straightforward project turn into a time sink for web developers. It is necessary to test websites in many

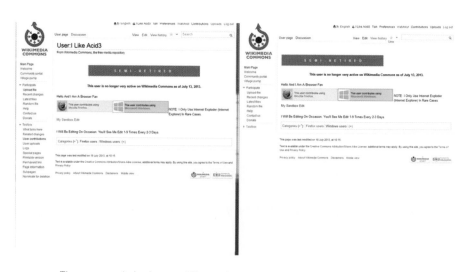

The same website in two different browsers

different browsers to ensure they are functioning properly in each one. If there are issues, additional code often has to be written.

As we saw previously, the ECMA sets the standards for what features browsers should support. According to their current data available online, the percentage of features that different browsers support varies widely. For instance, Opera and Chrome support 94 percent of ECMAScript 2016 (which JavaScript implements). However, Internet Explorer 11 supports just 3 percent, and Microsoft Edge 15 supports 76 percent.

If a feature on your website is unsupported by the browser of a viewer, it can interfere with the site's appearance and functionality. It is up to the developer to decide how much time to spend to make sure that a website functions in each and every browser that may be used to view it. These problems are compounded by the fact that many people use old versions of browsers that may support even fewer features.

There are a number of best practices that minimize the issues caused by some browsers. If you write code a certain way from the beginning, it can avoid many problems that may crop up later on. However, these practices take time and experience to learn. Writing code for individual browsers can solve many issues, but it also means your website will need to be updated constantly as new versions of browsers are released.

An Interpreted Language

The fact that JavaScript is an interpreted language comes with a variety of advantages and disadvantages. There are two kinds of programming languages: interpreted languages and compiled languages. Computers cannot execute code written in programming languages like JavaScript or C. Instead, the **source code** must first be interpreted or compiled before it can be executed.

Compiled languages are converted directly into bytecode, or machine code that the computer is capable of reading. Compiling is done up front before the code is executed and can be quite time-consuming for a complicated program. In contrast, interpreted languages are interpreted line by line and translated into instructions that the computer then runs. This means it takes less time for interpreted code to begin running, but in the long run interpretation can take longer because repetitive lines of code must be run through an interpreter every time they occur.

JIT (Just in Time) compilers are gaining traction with JavaScript and are included in modern browsers. These compile some JavaScript rather than always interpreting it. As a result, JavaScript executes faster than it used to when it was strictly an interpreted language.

The differences between interpreted and compiled languages matter when it comes to data types as well.

Data types are an important factor in what can and can't be done with a string, object, number, and more. For instance, code that tries to add a string (composed of text) to a number won't work. Compiled languages generally check data types when they compile the source code. They will notify the programmer of any errors before the code is even executed.

On the other hand, JavaScript does not check for data type errors until the code is actually being interpreted and run, at runtime. This means that a user may stumble upon an error before the programmer is even aware there is one. From a debugging perspective, there are pros and cons of both static type checking (during compilation) and dynamic type checking (during runtime). Static type checking makes it more likely a developer will find an error before a user; however, compiling your code can be a lengthy process, so debugging minor changes through static type checking can waste a great deal of time.

Speed of Development

It is possible to code quite quickly in JavaScript for a couple of reasons. This is a benefit compared to other languages where developers must spend more time at the beginning stages before getting started.

One reason it's easy to get started with JavaScript is because it is a weakly-typed language. This means

JSON versus XML

O O O

As discussed in the first chapter, Ajax is a key component of web development today. It allows the browser and server to communicate in the background, changing the website you are viewing without the need to reload it in its entirety. To do this, the browser and server exchange data.

Historically, the data exchanged by the server and web page was an XML file. (XML is a specific way of formatting data.) But in practice, the data is not always an XML file today. It is often in JSON (JavaScript Object Notation). JSON is more streamlined than XML and has gained in popularity in recent years. It is quicker for programmers to write and read it because similar statements written in both languages are shorter in JSON.

Here is an example of an array in JSON:

```
{"employees":[
    { "firstName":"Jane", "lastName":"Doe" },
    { "firstName":"John", "lastName":"Smith" },
    { "firstName":"Michael", "lastName":"Jones" }
]}
```

Compare it to the same data written in XML:

```
<employees>
  <employee>
    <firstName>Jane</firstName> <lastName>Doe</lastName>
  </employee>
  <employee>
    <firstName>John</firstName> <lastName>Smith</lastName>
  </employee>
  <employee>
    <firstName>Michael</firstName> <lastName>Jones</lastName>
  </employee>
</employees>
```

It is easy to see just how much shorter JSON is. This saves the programmer time when they are working. It also makes their code easier to understand at a glance. The JSON format is less cluttered with tags and numerous line breaks.

However, XML continues to be used by programmers instead of, or in addition to, JSON. It can accomplish some complicated tasks that JSON cannot. The important thing to note is that JSON heralds the rise of JavaScript not only as a client side and server side of web development but also as a format for data interchange between the two.

that you don't have to specify the data type of values. If you assign an object the value 5, JavaScript will assume it is a number. If you assign an object a value of "Hello world," it will assume it is a string. There is no need to write code stating what data type a value is. This is different from strongly-typed programming languages like C. In these languages, you must specify the data type of every value. Not having to do this makes coding JavaScript faster.

The downside of weakly-typed languages is that the data type still has to match what you are trying to do. If you try to add a number and a string in JavaScript, it will return an error and halt the process. It can also be more difficult for other people reading your code to figure out what is going on since the data type is always just implied and never stated.

Another reason that JavaScript is easy to get started with is that memory management is handled for you behind the scenes. While this is true of most languages, some still require you to handle how your program interacts with a device's memory. This can be a time-consuming process. With JavaScript, your script will use as much memory as it needs and then release it back to the system.

This results from a form of automatic memory management known as garbage collection. Garbage collection languages automate the process of removing objects that are no longer needed. This ensures there is no unnecessary drag on a computer's memory—and that the developer doesn't need to use their time writing code that governs memory management.

Some languages like C require the programmer to manage memory explicitly. This can be tricky to do well, and mistakes can harm the performance of your program. Therefore, it is much easier to jump right into coding with a language like JavaScript.

Chapter Four

Getting Started with JavaScript

Technology is one of the fastest-growing employment fields around the world. It is an exciting time to enter the sector. If you master a programming language like JavaScript, you can expect to earn a high salary for your expertise. It is also a relatively easy field to get started in, compared to other employment opportunities that require a license or certification, like health care and education.

Career and Salary Prospects

If you decide you want a coding job, the first question you have to ask yourself is what programming languages you will learn. In 2017, online developer community

Opposite: Many students begin learning to code in school. It is never too early to start!

Stack Overflow surveyed sixty-four thousand developers to see what languages professionals know. Unsurprisingly, JavaScript was the most commonly used programming language (for the fifth year in a row). Some 66.7 percent of professional developers reported using the language. This is a compelling reason to learn JavaScript—it is a requirement for the majority of programming jobs. No other programming language matches its popularity.

Furthermore, 72.6 percent of respondents to the survey identified themselves as web developers, making it by far the most popular role. Among web developers, knowledge of JavaScript is almost always necessary. Even if you plan on working on the server side, where JavaScript is not ubiquitous, some familiarity is useful.

One question you might have is how the salaries of developers who work in different languages compare. This is a difficult question to answer precisely because of the difficulty of gathering data on the salaries of so many people. Stack Exchange's survey relies on the self-reported income of respondents, but it is not a representative survey. Only 32 percent of respondents provided their salary. Among them, C++ proved the most lucrative language to know that is also used by more than 7 percent of programmers (more-obscure languages top the chart). The average annual salary for American developers who used C++ was self-reported at $100,890. This was followed closely by C at $100,000; Python at $99,000; Ruby at $97,000; Java at $96,000; and JavaScript at $90,000.

Another source, data taken from the popular job site Indeed.com, gives a somewhat different view. It has Ruby as the most highly compensated programming language at an average of $117,147. This is followed by Python at $116,027; C++ at $115,597; JavaScript at $110,062; Java at $102,043; and C at $95,045.

Ruby, Python, and C++ alternate among the top spots of both lists; however, the position of JavaScript varies greatly. This may be due to the fact that JavaScript is so flexible. Developers in many different roles, such as web development and app development, use the language. These roles sometimes have very different salary expectations.

Data from another job website, gooroo.io, makes this clear. The site breaks down what JavaScript developers make based on the framework they are responsible for using. According to their postings, the average salary of a developer who primarily uses Node.js is $98,003, while the average salary of one who uses React is $78,603. What you do with your knowledge of JavaScript can have a big impact on your salary.

To sum up, it is unclear what exactly a person who works with JavaScript could expect to earn compared to a peer who worked with another language like Ruby or C++. What is clear is that JavaScript is one of the most widely used programming languages, and it is popular among developers who work in many different fields in the tech industry.

More Motivation to Learn a Language

Outside of getting a job, there are other good reasons to learn how to program. Learning a programming language teaches you to think rationally and to solve problems. Many people have explained the myriad benefits that learning to code brings, and many influential people think all students should at least learn the basics of how to code to prepare them for life. In a 1995 interview, Apple founder Steve Jobs expressed his own views about why learning to program is so important:

> I think everybody in this country should learn how to program a computer, should learn a computer language, because it teaches you how to think. It's like going to law school. I don't think anybody should be a lawyer, but I think going to law school would actually be useful because it teaches you how to think in a certain way—in the same way, computer programming

Steve Jobs believed everyone should learn to code.

teaches you, in a slightly different way, how to think. I view computer science as a liberal art. It should be something everyone learns—takes a year in their life, one of the courses they take is learning how to program.

Once you've decided to learn how to code, the next question is how to go about it. The three main options are college, coding boot camp, or learning on your own. All three have their distinctive advantages and disadvantages, and which one is best for you is a highly personal choice. It depends on your preference for learning alone or in a group, as well as how much money you want to spend on education. College is by far the most expensive option (without significant scholarships), followed by coding boot camps, which can also cost thousands of dollars. Self-study, on the other hand, can be virtually free if you have a computer with internet access or can use one at a library.

The Question of College

One of the biggest decisions to make is whether or not to attend college to study a field related to coding, such as computer science or computer programming. This is a controversial question, and many people argue that you should get a degree in the field. Others say it is unnecessary and a waste of money given the high cost of tuition (and often four years outside the job market).

First, let's look at the arguments in favor of a degree. The fact is that the majority of professional developers have at least a bachelor's degree. According to the Stack Exchange survey, 76.5 percent of respondents did. Of these, almost 80 percent majored in a field related to computers. The numbers show that you'd be in good company if you decided to pursue a degree at college. Furthermore, more than a quarter of respondents reported having a master's or doctoral degree in the discipline. Traditional schooling is still quite popular in the industry.

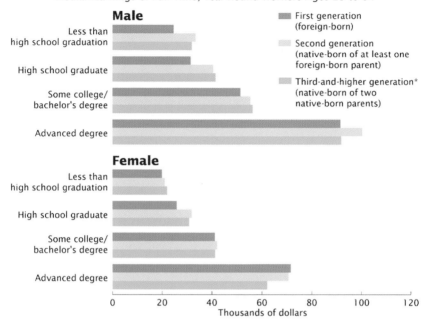

Generational Earnings and Education

Median Earnings of Full-Time, Year-Round Workers Ages 25 to 64

Male

- First generation (foreign-born)
- Second generation (native-born of at least one foreign-born parent)
- Third-and-higher generation* (native-born of two native-born parents)

Less than high school graduation

High school graduate

Some college/ bachelor's degree

Advanced degree

Female

Less than high school graduation

High school graduate

Some college/ bachelor's degree

Advanced degree

0   20   40   60   80   100   120
Thousands of dollars

Note: Refer to "Characteristics of the U.S. Population by Generational Status: 2013" for comparisons of the estimates. Data shown for 2012 reference year.
*Three quarters of the U.S. population were third-and-higher generation.

United States Census Bureau
census.gov

U.S. Department of Commerce
Economics and Statistics Administration
U.S. CENSUS BUREAU
census.gov

Source: 2013 Current Population Survey, Annual Social and Economic Supplement
www.census.gov/programs-surveys/cps.html

Salary tends to increase the more education you receive.

According to reports, employers often want to see a degree as well. According to a 2015 report by Burning Glass Technologies, an analytics software company that monitors the technology labor market, "89 percent of coding jobs typically require at least a bachelor's degree, compared to 44 percent of all career-track jobs." For the purposes of this report, career-track jobs are defined as those that pay more than $15 an hour.

Perhaps the most compelling reason to go to college is for your own education and enrichment. A bachelor's degree often requires a number of elective courses in the humanities and other fields. You might discover you are interested in some subjects you had never been exposed to before. Also, you will likely have to take a computer science class that covers the more theoretical aspects of computer science, such as how computing relates to mathematics.

Nevertheless, there are many people who say that a degree is not necessary for a successful career as a developer. The prominent examples for such arguments are often Bill Gates, the founder of Microsoft, and Steve Jobs, the founder of Apple. Neither one completed their own undergraduate studies (although they both began degrees). Instead, they left college to begin the work of starting their own companies that then went on to become two pillars of the tech industry.

One argument for not going to school to study programming is the fast-paced nature of the industry. Aspects of it, like what JavaScript framework is used to program apps, change at breakneck speed. By the time you finish a four-year degree program, it is likely that much of what you learned is hopelessly out of date.

Financial arguments are also put forward to argue against going to college. Salaries among those with degrees are typically slightly higher than among the self-taught. However, this difference drops off the further into one's career you look. And the fact of the matter is that a few thousand dollars a year does not offset the cost of school tuition and four years outside the job market in most cases.

Yale professor David Gelernter

Many people argue that the university courses themselves are out of touch with the real world and the job market. In 2015, a start-up head and Yale professor David Gelernter published an argument to this effect in the *Wall Street Journal* op-ed section:

The thing I don't look for in a developer is a degree in computer science. University computer science departments are in miserable shape: ten years behind in a field that changes every ten minutes. Computer science departments prepare their students for academic or research careers and spurn jobs that actually pay money.

They teach students how to design an operating system, but not how to work with a real, live development team.

There isn't a single course in iPhone or Android development in the computer science departments of Yale or Princeton. Harvard has one, but you can't make a good developer in one term.

In the end, whether or not to attend college is a personal choice. There are good arguments both for and against it. Even if you do go to college, you will likely have to teach yourself a number of skills to be a marketable developer. If you decide not to go to college, there are other options to look at.

Boot Camps

Coding boot camps—crash courses in how to code—are a controversial subject. The programs typically last from two to six months and aim to prepare students for an entry-level job in the field of computer programming or web development. JavaScript is a popular programming language, among many others, for boot camps to cover since it is so common.

In the past, boot camps have been endorsed by many notable people such as President Obama. It was hoped that they might both prepare unemployed people for work and fill the shortage of computer programmers in the United States. However, because many boot camps are for-profit, expensive, and do not always lead to employment, their reputation has declined over time.

The primary benefit of a coding boot camp is its short time frame. A computer science degree takes years to complete. Alternatively, a boot camp takes just weeks or months. As a result, boot camps are less expensive, although tuitions can still be quite steep. On the other hand, the short time frame means students are not able to spend as much time learning. This has led to numerous controversies.

Some boot camps have come under fire for not adequately preparing their students to find a job in the real world. Despite charging thousands or tens of thousands of dollars in tuition, graduates may not be prepared to pass a coding test or succeed in a job interview. Some graduates have successfully sued boot camps they attended for not teaching them the skills they advertised. Other graduates have been left without a job and with tens of thousands of dollars in debt.

However, many boot camps do prepare their students for finding a job. Some do not even require you to pay for the cost of the program unless you manage to find a job. As with all levels of education, there is a great deal of disparity in the quality of coding boot camps.

If you decide to look into attending a boot camp, you should make sure to review their statistics regarding what percentage of students finish the program on time, find a job soon after graduation, and what their starting salary is. This information should be available from a neutral third party and not just the boot camp itself. In the past, some boot camps have been forced to shut down due to misleading and false statistics they used to advertise their services. The Council on Integrity in Results Reporting (CIRR) publishes data for a number of coding boot camps online.

Learning Alone

There are many resources for learning a programming language like JavaScript on your own. Local libraries and school libraries often have materials for self-study. You can learn how the language works and how to write code.

However, the most common way to learn a programming language on your own is online. There are countless free websites that teach the basics of JavaScript and other programming languages. One good website for learning is w3schools.com. It walks you through learning HTML and CSS, as well as JavaScript. Once you know these three languages, it is possible to design your own simple websites.

W3schools.com is one available resource for learning to code online.

From there, you need to learn more about various JavaScript libraries and frameworks. While tools like Node.js and React are primarily written in JavaScript, they have their own quirks that you need to learn. It is these more advanced tools that make it possible to create sleek websites in a short timeframe. Coding everything yourself in just HTML, CSS, and JavaScript is a time-consuming process, and it forces you to find solutions to common problems that can easily be solved by a JavaScript framework or library.

It's useful to have your own computer when you do this so that you can write code and see if it works. If you're working on front-end web development, you just need a browser installed on the computer. If you're working on the back end, you will also need Node.js. To create apps, you'll need to download a framework before you can get started.

Tech Jobs

The demand for software developers and web developers is growing rapidly. You have likely heard of the emphasis on STEM (science, technology, engineering, and mathematics) both in school systems and in the work force. It is a hot topic today in education and in politics, as the labor market changes and highly skilled workers with knowledge of these four subjects are in high demand.

According to the US Department of Labor, the average job is expected to experience 7 percent growth between 2014 and 2024. However, the number of software developers is expected to grow 17 percent, while the number of web developers is expected to grow 27 percent! This is great news if you want to become a software developer. It is likely you will be able to find a job in your chosen field. Salaries are also likely to be high due to the high demand and limited supply for workers in the field.

Correspondent John Dodge, writing for the *Boston Globe*, discussed how the shortage of software developers in Massachusetts was affecting the state in 2016:

> How fierce is the competition for technical talent in Massachusetts?
> Software developers right out of college can command starting salaries of up to $90,000.

Pathways After a Bachelor's Degree in

Computers and Math

Educational Attainment, Common Occupations, and
Synthetic Work-Life Earnings Estimates

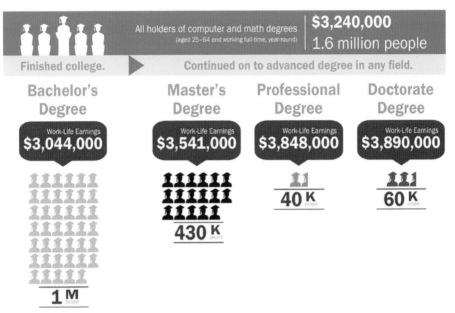

Lifetime earnings in the tech field are affected by your exact job title as well as your educational level.

Once in their jobs, they can get as many as twenty recruiting calls a day trying to convince them to leave for another company. And when they do, a 20 percent to 25 percent bump in salary is not unusual.

The shortage of skilled technology workers has become the No. 1 issue for many Massachusetts companies and a growing concern for the state's innovation economy. Tech executives describe the hiring environment as brutal—worse even than the dot-com boom in the late 1990s—and a threat to their ability to expand, develop new technologies, and keep growing.

While this article focuses on Massachusetts, the same issues confront companies around the country and the globe.

Fears about Outsourcing

Since the 1990s, there have been fears that outsourcing—having an outside company take over some task—would lead to a scarcity of jobs in the United States as companies moved more and more jobs overseas. Luckily, this fear was unfounded. While some jobs have been moved overseas, most remain in the United States. The draw of cheaper labor costs due to lower wages in some countries has not been able to outweigh the numerous drawbacks of outsourcing overseas.

The fear of outsourcing was perhaps most intense in the tech world. In 2008, tech author Steve Holzner wrote an article detailing just how widespread the worries about outsourcing were in the tech field—both at companies and in universities. He cited dropping enrollment numbers in computer science programs around the country and pessimism among programmers that they might soon lose their jobs. However, as Holzner said at the time, fears were overblown. While outsourcing is a relevant issue for economies around the world, the tech sector continues to boom in the United States.

The US Department of Labor projections provide an interesting snapshot of this issue. According to their figures, the number of computer programmers in the United States is projected to *decline* 8 percent between 2014 and 2024—a shocking fact given the average career is expected to grow 7 percent. The US Department of Labor explains this is the result of the fact that "Computer programming can be done from anywhere in the world, so companies sometimes hire programmers in countries where wages are lower."

At first glance, outsourcing overseas seems to be a discouraging prospect. However, upon closer inspection, this is not the case. The number of software developers (as opposed to computer programmers) is expected to increase 17 percent. Furthermore, the average salary of a software developer was $102, 280 in 2016, compared to an average salary of $79,840 for computer engineers. While the lower-paid work is being lost to companies overseas, more highly compensated work in the same sector is growing quickly in the United States. Most likely, this is due to the fact that work that requires collaboration (and is best done in the country) is also typically higher paying than work that can be done in isolation—and can be outsourced easily.

Silicon Valley

Tech jobs can be found all over the United States and the world. However, there are some regions that are particularly important in the sector. This means it may be easier to find jobs in these locations, since there are so many companies seeking employees. It also means that people trying to rise to the top of the field often move to these areas to give themselves the most opportunities for advancement.

The states with the most computer programmers are California, Texas (home to Dallas), New York, Illinois (home to Chicago), and New Jersey. One reason for these groupings is the large population in these states, but they are also home to important tech centers. Cities like New York City (and nearby New Jersey), Chicago, and Dallas, as well as San Francisco and Los Angeles in California are full of tech companies. Computer programmers often move to these cities to find employment and sometimes relocate among them because many companies have offices in more than one of them.

Silicon Valley is home to numerous leading tech companies.

But in tech, no place is as famous as Silicon Valley—an area in California's San Francisco Bay Area. It is the undisputed king of the tech industry, and its name is known around the world. Many of the biggest names in the industry are headquartered in Silicon Valley, including Google, Apple, and Facebook.

Silicon Valley has played an important role in the history of computing. It gained its name in 1971 based on the concentration of electronics manufacturers in the region. Silicon is used to make the chips that make electronics like phones and computers run. But even before 1971, the region played an integral role in the tech sector.

Silicon Valley's prominence is largely due to the fact that Stanford University is located in its heart. A professor, and later dean and provost, of Stanford

University by the name of Frederick Terman played a large role in efforts to make the valley a center of technology. In 1939, two of Terman's former students, William Hewlett and David Packard, founded Hewlett-Packard (HP) in a garage in the valley with Terman's encouragement. Today, HP sells nearly 20 percent of all personal computers in the world. While HP was the first company founded by Stanford graduates in the region, it was not the last. Google and Yahoo! would follow it years later, and Stanford continues to be a leader of the industry.

Silicon Valley is not only home to the headquarters of many of the biggest and well-established tech companies, it is also the place with the most start-ups in the world. Start-ups generally rely on money that is given to them by rich investors or investment banks to get off the ground. This allows them to create their product and pay their employees' salaries while they work on their initial product. This initial investment in companies that do not offer stock is called **venture capital**.

Venture capital can often be substantial. For instance, just a few months after its founding in 2004, Facebook received $500,000 from an **angel investor**. At the time, the company was quite small and still run by university students. The company went on to receive much more capital over the years. Most notably, in 2011 the investment bank Goldman Sachs invested $450 million in Facebook—a staggering sum.

If you decide to try to launch a start-up and are looking for venture capital, there is no better place than Silicon Valley. An astounding 25 percent of the world's venture capital— more than $10 billion in 2012—is invested in Silicon Valley. In fact, Silicon Valley sees more venture capital investment than the entire continent of Europe.

This influx of huge sums of money into the region also has its drawbacks. Property values and the cost of living in Silicon Valley are extraordinarily high. This is something to keep in mind if you are offered a job in the area. The median home price in Silicon Valley is about $1 million dollars. For comparison, the median home price in Chicago is less than $300,000. While salaries in Silicon Valley are higher than Chicago on average, it's not enough to offset the huge difference in housing costs.

Nevertheless, netting a job in Silicon Valley remains the dream of many computer programmers. While entry-level employees don't get paid enough to lead glamorous lifestyles in the expensive area, successful start-up founders and senior employees at large companies can bring home impressive salaries.

Electron and GitHub

○ ○ ○

One of the most recent innovations in the world of JavaScript is the ability to easily create desktop applications for computers using the language. This is largely due to the new framework called Electron that began in 2013 (under the name Atom Shell). Electron makes it possible to create desktop apps for computers running Windows, Mac, and Linux operating systems. You can write the code in JavaScript (as well as HTML and CSS), and the resulting program looks like a native computer application.

There are many desktop apps that have been built with Electron. WordPress, a popular platform for easily creating websites, has an application that was built with Electron, and Discord—a popular voice and text communication app used by gamers—was also made with it. Electron itself was developed by the start-up GitHub.

GitHub is a cloud-based service that stores code. Individuals and businesses can purchase memberships that allow them to store their programs and code. The benefits of this are that GitHub simplifies the process of many people working on the same code. It lets you set access controls and aids the process of collaboration. Users can request that other people review their code—this provides them with feedback and improves the final product.

These features not only benefit businesses, but also the many open-source projects that developers rely on to do their work. Many JavaScript libraries and frameworks are open-source projects. Countless developers who use them in their work also contribute to them online so that they function better for everyone. If you need to download a JavaScript framework like React, you can often do it on GitHub. Once you've learned how to code, you can also propose changes to improve open-source projects like React on GitHub—this can be a good way to build your résumé.

Electron also benefits from being open source. According to GitHub's website:

> Electron 1.0 is the result of a community effort by hundreds of developers. Outside of the core framework, there have been hundreds of libraries and tools released to make building, packaging, and deploying Electron apps easier.
>
> There is now a new community page that lists many of the awesome Electron tools, apps, libraries, and frameworks being developed. You can also check out the Electron and Electron Userland organizations to see some of these fantastic projects.

GitHub is an extremely important website for developers around the world. As of May 2017, Amazon's Alexa estimates that it is the forty-sixth most popular website in the United States, and the sixty-third most popular in the entire world. This is due to the fact that millions of programmers and developers use it on a regular basis. If you spend much time coding, it is almost certain that you will use GitHub and its many resources for developers—it's not necessary to pay for a membership unless you want to host your own private projects there.

Jobs and JavaScript

Once you know how to code in JavaScript, a wide variety of career options open up. One of the first choices you need to make is whether to go into web development or not. Web development is focused on the creation of websites. Often, web developers will have some experience with graphic design since they may be responsible for designing the layout of the website as well as the functional, technical aspects of it.

One noteworthy fact about web development is that it has a high number of **self-employed** individuals working in it. In 2014, approximately one in seven web developers were self-employed, meaning they work for themselves or run their own business rather than work for a company.

Self-employment has a number of advantages and drawbacks. One of its most appealing aspects is that you don't have a boss if you are self-employed. You can create your own schedule and set your own hours. However, this also means that you are responsible for finding your own clients. You need to market yourself to find paying work, and you still do answer to your clients even if they are not your boss. Furthermore, you have to motivate yourself to do your work; the fact that no one is setting your hours can quickly become a problem if you procrastinate.

Landing a Job

If you decide to look for a job rather than strike out as a **freelancer**, you need to work on perfecting your résumé and honing your skills. Generally, large companies like Google or Facebook require a strong computer science background. While you might send off an application, you should also look at smaller companies that have more relaxed standards if you taught yourself or went to a coding boot camp. In general, small starts-ups are the most willing to give self-taught programmers a chance.

To improve your chance of landing a job, you can take a number of steps. The most important is to practice coding and programming. Even if you went to a boot camp or graduated with a degree in computer science, it is important to refine your skills and prepare for coding tests—they are often part of the hiring process. Interviewers will often ask questions to test your knowledge, and time spent coding and learning how to code is time well spent.

Getting involved in projects on GitHub is a great way to show off your coding skills.

Steve Jobs (*left*) and Steve Wozniak (*right*) started Apple in a garage.

You can also build your résumé by working on projects even before you are hired for your first job. If there are apps or websites you built on your own to add to your résumé, this demonstrates your ability to code and your talent. Additionally, you can contribute to open-source projects online to show that you are a capable programmer. Adding accomplishments like this to your résumé can be especially important if you are self-taught. It is proof that your skills are up to par and you would make a valuable addition to a programming team.

In addition to these programming-specific tips, it is also important to follow general advice for seeking a job. You should make sure your résumé is polished and proofread. Employers want to know that you are attentive to details and take pride in your work. Also, networking is important in the programming world just as in any other field. Many people get jobs when they hear about them from a friend or acquaintance.

Perhaps the most important thing is to keep trying to find a job. Most openings have dozens of applicants, so it is necessary to keep trying even if you don't find one right away. Programming is in such high demand that if your skills are sharp, you can find a job eventually if you keep trying and practicing coding.

JavaScript: The Language that Changed the Web

Since its creation in 1995, JavaScript has been an integral language for computer programmers. Its development resulted in interactive web pages, which spurred the modern growth of the web and led to the collaborative, social web that we know today. Since then, its usage has also expanded into app creation and other domains of programming. Its reach is unmatched by any other programming language, and virtually all professional programmers have some knowledge of JavaScript. Nevertheless, it is a powerful language and mastering it—and its popular frameworks and libraries—is a difficult task.

Yet with some effort and practice, mastery is a possibility for all kinds of learners. The payoffs of learning JavaScript are huge. Fluency in the language truly opens doors to a wide range of careers. It also gives you the opportunity to leave your mark on the web.

angel investor A wealthy individual who gives a large amount of money to a start-up or individual entrepreneur.

AngularJS A popular JavaScript Framework that is designed to create single-page web applications.

array In JavaScript, a kind of variable that can hold more than one value.

back end The part of the website that your browser communicates with over the internet. It consists of the server and sometimes databases and applications. It is also known as the server side.

Boolean A data type that stores the information "true" or "false."

callback A JavaScript function used to order when lines of code will execute.

compatible Two or more items that can work together.

data type A classification of data; common data types are numbers and strings (of characters, generally words or sentences).

elements In HTML, elements are individual components of the HTML document. They often have start and end tags, such as \<p\> and \</p\> for a paragraph, but sometimes they are one tag, such as \<br\> for a line break.

encrypted The quality of being encoded for security reasons.

framework JavaScript frameworks structure your code and are intended to simplify some processes so that you can focus on the content of your website or app rather than writing code.

freelancer A person who is self-employed rather than the employee of a company.

front end The part of a website that is visible to the user and often changes based on their input. It is also called the client side.

library JavaScript libraries are collections of pre-written code that can help developers save time. They are generally less all-encompassing than frameworks.

methods In JavaScript, methods are actions that can be performed on objects.

native Native code is designed to run on a particular system—making it faster. Code that isn't native tends to run slower.

open source The source code of open-source software is freely available and people are allowed to modify it. There are often communities that maintain and improve popular open-source software.

operating system The software responsible for a computer or smartphone's basic functionality.

properties The values associated with a JavaScript object; for example, if the object is a vehicle, the properties could be its weight and color.

React A JavaScript library created by Facebook that primarily deals with the user interface of web pages.

React Native A JavaScript framework created by Facebook that allows users to create Android and iOS applications using JavaScript.

referendum A direct vote by the people on a single political issue, rather than the typical legislative process of representatives voting on a law.

runtime The time period when a computer program executes.

scripting language A programming language that executes commands at runtime.

self-employed Working as a freelancer or small business owner rather than as an employee of another person or business.

source code Instructions for a computer that can be understood by people.

spaghetti code An informal and pejorative phrase for code that is needlessly complex and difficult to work with as a result of poor programming.

start-up A new business that hopes to grow quickly and usually has outside funding.

static Unchanging.

strings A set of characters that can include letters and numbers. It is a common data type that is used to store words and sentences.

syntax The "grammar" of a programming language.

third-party Developed by an outside company.

UI User interface; the part of a website or application that the user interacts with. It includes the display as well as the means of interaction, such as the cursor and input fields.

venture capital Money invested in a start-up in exchange for a percentage of the business.

‹Further Information/›

Books

Freeman, Eric T., and Elisabeth Robson. *Head First JavaScript Programming: A Brain-Friendly Guide.* Sebastopol, CA: O'Reilly Media Inc., 2014.

McFarland, David Sawyer. *JavaScript and jQuery: The Missing Manual.* Sebastopol, CA: O'Reilly Media Inc., 2014.

Minnick, Chris, and Eva Holland. *Coding with JavaScript for Dummies.* Hoboken: Wiley, 2015.

Websites

Codecademy

https://www.codecademy.com

Codecademy is one of the many free services online that aims to teach beginners how to code. JavaScript is one language that is covered.

GitHub Tutorial: Intro to React

https://facebook.github.io/react/tutorial/tutorial.html

Learn how to build an interactive tic-tac-toe game using React.

Mozilla Development Network: JavaScript Basics

https://developer.mozilla.org/en-US/docs/Learn/
Getting_started_with_the_web/JavaScript_basics

Mozilla provides a thorough look at the basics of JavaScript at the beginning of their guide on the language.

Videos

"JavaScript Fundamentals for Beginners"

https://www.youtube.com/watch?v=vEROU2XtPR8

Traversy Media explains the fundamentals of JavaScript and programming in general.

"JavaScript Tutorial"

https://www.youtube.com/watch?v=fju9ii8YsGs

Derek Banas presents an in-depth tutorial of JavaScript.

<Bibliography/>

AngularJS. "What Is AngularJS?" Retrieved June 10, 2017. https://docs.angularjs.org/guide/introduction.

BBC. "New Ransomware Strain Coded Entirely in JavaScript." June 20, 2016. http://www.bbc.com/news/technology-36575687.

Dodge, John. "The War for Tech Talent Escalates." *Boston Globe*, February 19, 2016. https://www.bostonglobe.com/business/2016/02/19/the-war-for-tech-talent-escalates/ejUSbuPCjPLCMRYIRZIKoJ/story.html.

Florida, Richard. "The Global Cities Where Tech Venture Capital Is Concentrated." *Atlantic*, January 26, 2016.

Garrett, Jesse James. "Ajax: A New Approach to Web Applications." Adaptive Path, February 18, 2005. http://adaptivepath.org/ideas/ajax-new-approach-web-applications/.

Herlihy, Peter. "How Many People Are Missing Out on JavaScript Enhancement?" Government Digital Service Blog, October 21, 2013. https://gds.blog.gov.uk/2013/10/21/how-many-people-are-missing-out-on-javascript-enhancement/.

Holzner, Steve. "Why Outsourcing is Scaring Off Potential CS Students." *Tech Republic*, September 15, 2008. http://www.techrepublic.com/blog/software-engineer/why-outsourcing-is-scaring-off-potential-cs-students/.

Metz, Rachel. "Apple Seeks a Swift Way to Lure More Developers." *MIT Technology Review*, June 3, 2014. https://

www.technologyreview.com/s/527821/apple-seeks-a-swift-way-to-lure-more-developers/.

National Research Council (US) Committee on Competing in the 21st Century. *Best Practices in State and Regional Innovation Initiatives: Competing in the 21st Century.* Washington, DC: National Academies Press, 2013.

Naughton, John. "Netscape: The Web Browser that Came Back to Haunt Microsoft." *Guardian,* March 22, 2015. https://www.theguardian.com/global/2015/mar/22/web-browser-came-back-haunt-microsoft.

O'Reilly, Tim. "What is Web 2.0." O'Reilly, September 30, 2005. http://www.oreilly.com/pub/a/web2/archive/what-is-web-20.html?page=1.

Roberts, Jeff John. "This App Guy Thinks Computer Science Degrees Are a Waste of Money." *Fortune*, September 1, 2015. http://fortune.com/2015/09/01/computer-science-degree/.

Smith, Aaron. "Record Shares of Americans Now Own Smartphones, Have Home Broadband." Pew Research Center, January 12, 2017. http://www.pewresearch.org/fact-tank/2017/01/12/evolution-of-technology/.

Surowiecki, James. "How Mozilla Lost its C.E.O." *New Yorker*, April 4, 2014. http://www.newyorker.com/business/currency/how-mozilla-lost-its-c-e-o.

Thibodeau, Patrick. "U.S. Expects Drop in Programming Jobs, But Gains in IT Jobs Overall." *Computer World*, December 22, 2015. http://www.computerworld.com/article/3017672/it-careers/u-s-expects-drop-in-programming-jobs-but-gains-in-it-jobs-overall.html.

Page numbers in **boldface** are illustrations. Entries in **boldface** are glossary terms.

Facebook, 20, 24–25, 28–29, 42, 50–51, 55, 59–60, 93–95, 99

framework, 65–66, 77, 82, 87–88, 96–97, 101

freelancer, 99

front end, 31–32, 39, 41, 55–56, 60–61, 87

Gates, Bill, 7, **8**, 82

GitHub, 96–97, **99**

Google, 19, 23, 26, 39–40, 42–44, 93–94, 99

HTML, 14–19, **16**, 27, 32–34, 39, 44–46, 61–64, 87, 96

Integrated Development Environment (IDE), 38–39, **38**

internet, 5–7, 11–15, 22, 34, 38, 44, 48, 54

Internet Explorer, 7–8, 12–13, 16, 26, 67

interpreted languages, 68

iPhone, **22**, 23, 84

Java, 9, 26–27, 31, 41, 50, 56, 61, 77

Jobs, Steve, 78, **79**, 82, **100**

jQuery, 44, **65**

library, 24, 41–42, 44–47, 50, 56, 65–66, 80, 86–87, 96–97, 101

Linux, 96

malware, 48–49

MEAN stack, **60**, 61, 65

methods, 35–36

Microsoft, 7–9, 12–13, 41, 67, 82

mobile application, 26–27

Mozilla, 10–11

native, 27–29, 96

Netscape, 7–10, 12–13

Netscape Navigator, 7, **9**, 10, 13, 16, 26

Node.js, 41, 51, 61, 77, 87–88

Objective-C, 26–27, 29, 50

open source, 10, 44, 55, 66, 96–97

operating system, 8, 23, 26–27, 42, 50, 84, 96

O'Reilly, Tim, 20–21

<About the Author/>

Derek Miller is a writer and educator from Salisbury, Maryland. He writes about science, history, and technology. His many books include *Henry David Thoreau: Civil Disobedience* and *Earth, Sun, and Moon: Cyclic Patterns of Lunar Phases, Eclipses, and the Seasons*. He enjoys traveling with his wife and tackling programming projects in JavaScript.

$29.95

LONGWOOD PUBLIC LIBRARY
800 Middle Country Road
Middle Island, NY 11953
(631) 924-6400
longwoodlibrary.org

LIBRARY HOURS

Monday-Friday	9:30 a.m. - 9:00 p.m.
Saturday	9:30 a.m. - 5:00 p.m.
Sunday (Sept-June)	1:00 p.m. - 5:00 p.m.